Thirst Quenched: A Woman at the Well

Marcia Riggs Hawkins

Foreword by: Dr. Gina A. McDaniel

ROYSTON
Publishing

BK Royston Publishing
P. O. Box 4321
Jeffersonville, IN 47131
502-802-5385
http://www.bkroystonpublishing.com
bkroystonpublishing@gmail.com

© Copyright – 2017

All Rights Reserved. No part of this book may be reproduced, stored in a retrieval system, or transmitted by any means without the written permission of the author.

Cover Design: Brent Barnett for besquareddesigns.com
Photo Credit: Demond L. Smalls of Smalls Photography

ISBN-10: 1-946111-25-2
ISBN-13: 978-1-946111-25-8

Printed in the United States of America

Dedication

This book is dedicated to the memory of my parents, James and Virginia Riggs and my loving husband, Keith Hawkins.

Foreword

As I look into the beautiful sunset the Creator of the Universe the Omniscient God appears to show off his craftwork. Facets of rays bounce off the downy clouds as they dance in the sky. Sea gulls sing as they soar over the horizon. The gentle breeze cause the tree branches to dance ever so gently. As my eyes scan the sky and all its beauty and as my ears bear witness to the songs of Gods flying creatures. In all the Glory of God it is only one individual I personally know who could capture every site and every sound and put the pen to canvas and allow what I see in the moment to last forever. That person is one of my closest friends, Marcia Gordon Hawkins.

Marcia and I are so close we address each other as "skin". She is the first person I talk to in the morning, "Good Morning skin". I cheerfully reply, Good Morning skin, thank God for another day. The love I have for Marcia is like a twin sister on days and other days it's like a being her big sister as we try to contemplate and navigate through life situations only to come to the final conclusion that God is in control.

Marica has a gift which exhumes her essence. She has the God given aptitude to paint pictures and stories with words. Her analogies of life situations and world views will draw others into the world with a complete understanding of the similarities of the two features.

Marica's book Woman at the Well is a collection of the well-crafted words which capture so many life circumstances. Like the woman at the well Jesus was able to tell her all the mysteries of her life. So it is with Marcia's poetry, the reader will find themselves so engulfed in the words that soon they are in the very midst of every vivid description unmasking the mystery of the poetry.

Gina A. McDaniel

Preface

This compilation of writings has been the result of lessons learned and some disappointments. The one thing that has been consistent thru it all, is the love of Jesus, and knowing that I can do all things thru Christ.

Some experiences, even if they are painful, give you a growth that you wouldn't receive if you didn't have the lesson.

My release of dealing with my hurts have been my writings, and I pray through that these passages of readings will help someone else, as it helped me to release it on paper. Whatever your situation, you are not alone. Someone else really does understand.

I thank God for these special women in my life, who inspired me, listened to me, prayed with me and nurtured me; Marissa Riggs-Cathcart, Gina McDaniel, Marilyn Joyner; my spiritual mother, Pat Lambert, and someone who will always be dear to my heart, Carolyn Ford.

Marcia Riggs Hawkins

John 4:4 - "Greater is He that is in You, than He that is in the world."

Table of Contents

Dedication	iii
Foreword	v
Preface	vii
A Bad Dream	1
A Balm in My Gilead	3
A Day Without God	5
A Figment of an Imaginative Imagination	7
THE Addiction	9
BEAUTIFUL BLACK MAN	11
Dear Father,	13
Dear Heavenly Father	15
Dear Jesus	17
Deceit	19
Deep Pain	21
The Definition of Me	23
Don't Judge Me	25
Erase	27
False Hope	29
Feel Me	31
The Frailty of Broken Limbs.	33
God,	37
Going Back to Bring one Forward	39

Happily Ever Dreams	41
Harvest	43
He Stepped Out of My Mind	45
He's Waiting	47
How I Feel	49
Hurt, Pain, Loneliness, Despair	51
I Am the Prize	53
I Smile	55
Lord I'm Calling on You...	57
My Other Sista	59
My Thickness	61
Our Story	63
Queen	67
Reclaiming Myself	69
Thank You	71
Unconditional	73
Under Construction	75
Untimely Cravings of Course	77
When You Look at me, What Do You Really See?	79
Where am I?	81
White Horses and Fairy Tales	83
Winning	85
Woman at the Well	87
The Woman You Trained	91

Words	93
Your Will/My Purpose	95

THIRST QUENCHED:

A WOMAN AT THE WELL

Thirst Quenched: Woman at the Well

A Bad Dream

I went to sleep four years ago.

I dreamt of a man who was about 6'2, or so.

He was charming and innocent, or so it seemed.

How could I know he would be nothing but a bad dream?
I believed in love, second chances and redemptive souls.

I believed in fairy tales, white horses and knights of long ago.
As life progressed with this so-called prince, he brought hurt, pain, mistrust and guilt.
Tears that wouldn't dry from eyes that, after some time, refused to cry.

Emotions sucked out like life, left to dissipate, and the evilness of hate smeared on my pillow like a made up face.
I tossed and fought, and awoke from this mess.

The veil was lifted, and I felt like a wreck!

I checked to see if I was intact.

See, I'd just come from hell and back!

Everything looked ok, had no missing parts, then I looked down on my pillow, and saw pieces of my heart.
How could I survive such an awful dream?

Because God's grace is new, and new mercies I see.
No longer do I lay with pain on my pillow, or residues of hurt.

It doesn't have to be a place where I harvest pain, my bed to lay down, and let life drain, ebbed from my soul, until it exists no more.
It's been removed, wiped away by Gods amazing love.

My pillow is now a gateway to sweet rest.

Now, I lay me down to sleep.

Thirst Quenched: Woman at the Well

A Balm in My Gilead

He is my balm in Gilead, my healing ointment, my antibiotic cure.

Every touch of his hands, his arms, his eyes, and his breath penetrates my open wounds and scars of past tears, saturating them with love so deep and sincere that all that is left is the residue left on my pillow once stained with the pain and hurt but I rise and leave it behind because the man is mine, and I can dream his words like the balm, calm, resound like melodies that linger in my head. His love, healing to me, and I love the way he loves.

I'm glad God created me as woman, his woman.

The better half to my other half.

Marcia Riggs Hawkins

A Day Without God

A day without God, well, what would that be? Let's see.

My slumber would be restless from the peace that I would lack.

(GOD IS A GOD OF PERFECT PEACE)

I realize things were not as I left them.

Everything is out of order, chaos in the air. Oh, God, I wanna pull my hair.

(GOD IS NOT A GOD OF CONFUSION)

Yet I trudge on because I'm gonna have a day without God.

Journeying through the day, trials will befall my every step.

There's nowhere to turn, and destruction is in my path

(GOD IS A PROTECTOR)

Here I am, feeling scared and all alone

(HE PROMISED NEVER TO LEAVE, NEVER TO LEAVE YOU ALONE)

Marcia Riggs Hawkins

Without God in my day all seems so dark

(JESUS IS THE LIGHT OF THE WORLD)

No good ending in sight. I'm gonna pray to my Savior, pray with all my might.

Please God, I don't wanna see another minute separated from thee

(JUST A CLOSER WALK WITH THEE, GRANT IT JESUS, IF YOU PLEASE)

I invite You in, please come right now.

A day without God? No, that's not for me.

I need my Savior for eternity.
I won't spend another moment without Your holy presence

(I NEED THEE, OH, I NEED THEE)

A Figment of an Imaginative Imagination

When I met you, I think my imagination was working overtime.

I could have sworn you said something about forever.

Maybe I was wrong, or you were wronged...

But, I remembered thinking that you were too good to be true.

How could you know everything I needed and wanted, and yet just be a figment, of
my overactive imagination?
It was like the character in my dreams had become real.

He did and said everything I wanted, but yet, he wasn't...

He wasn't just part of my imaginative imagination.

He was part of a dream that worked me up into a nightmare.

I tried to go back to sleep and dream a different ending,

But I couldn't, because you see...none of this was real.

It was all imagined. It was a dream that turned into a nightmare, so wake up!

Wake up!!!

Wipe the sleep out of your eyes and see it for what it is...

It's someone from your imagination who should've stayed...in your imaginary world.

Once he left that world and came into your own then the reality became clear.

All he said, and all he did, was just imaginary.

It was just my imagination, running away with me...

THE ADDICTION

Another broken promise, another shattered dream. All because I chose to believe that you wanted me more than her.

She gets you high, makes you paranoid, takes all your money and makes you look and smell like a fool. She robs your children and makes you support a household where you don't even live.

And yet, you give, give, and give, until all you have left is what's in your back; she sends you home. Back to the dream she shattered.

Back to the promises that came out of your mouth but not your heart. Back to the one that took your hand in marriage while you took her spleen, you see, 'cause when you got her, nothing else matters.

Life, death, disaster and destruction could occur. When she's finished with you, discarded you will be.

Marcia Riggs Hawkins

Like the thousands before and after you, your legacy will be will be more than the life.

The stone that will read, "wonderful talent, gentle soul; too bad, he couldn't let it go."

Thirst Quenched: Woman at the Well

BEAUTIFUL BLACK MAN

His hair coarse as it may be, protects the mind and thoughts of what he hopes to be. His face shines from the sweat mixed in with the hues…

That God has blessed him with, and he's not ashamed of the richness that covers him.

His neck is so thick, maybe from work or maybe, it's what his daddy gave him,

But its purpose is for my hands, my lips, my face to rest upon....

They're for me to find peace and to rest on. What shoulders he has! They have carried his burdens, and my burdens.

They connect to those arms. Oh, those arms.

The same ones that wrap me close, hold me tight, and handle me with care.
His trunk is broad because God knew he would work.

By the sweat of his brow he would work.

It also encases a beautiful heart that pumps by God's rhythm.

It helps God's love circulate throughout his being.

His legs are like that of a wonderful stallion.

They allow him to stand erect, tall, and bulletproof!

Legs to walk with pride and run for grace.

They stand for something and fall for nothing!

With all that God created in him he loves me like he loves his soul.

He caresses me with his eyes, and his breath is likes God's breath, breathing into my lungs.

With his kiss, his lips make me forget.

God created him so beautifully, and out of his rib I come to serve him, to stand by him, and to hold him…

When the world wants to let him go.
My beautiful black man, how I love thee.

I've already counted the ways.

Thirst Quenched: Woman at the Well

Dear Father

How in my human mind, can I imagine someone loving me so much that He bore my sins on a cross that should've been for me?

How can someone love me in spite of me, not be ashamed of me in the presence of His Father, and prove His love for me, over and over again?

Even when I don't always acknowledge Him, He still insists to You that I'm worthy of salvation.

I thank You, God, that His blood was enough to pay the price for me.

Thank You for salvation and mercies being new every day for me.

That alone is enough to give you all glory and honor, but then You turn around and bless me!

That's when my praise turns to Hallelujah because you didn't give me what I deserved.

Thank you, Master.

Continue to bless and keep us for Your glory....

Thirst Quenched: Woman at the Well

Dear Heavenly Father

Today, God, my mind just goes to Your Son.

How could someone love me so much that He bore a cross that was meant for me? That with each drop of blood that should've been mine, he shed just for me?

I'm overwhelmed that someone loves me that much, and still insists on giving me grace even when I don't deserve it.

He petitions You, Father, on my behalf. He comes to my rescue when I get into situations where I knew better, and He doesn't throw it back in my face.

He just wants me to repent and follow Him. My bridegroom; the ultimate lover of man. The one who washed me clean with His precious blood.

Thank You, Father, for giving me Life through Jesus.

I love you, God.

Marcia Riggs Hawkins

Thirst Quenched: Woman at the Well

Dear Jesus

Jesus, even in my drunken state of false love, and lust, even in my perpetual quest for something that's not real, you still love me.

When I look to the anthill, instead of looking to the hills,

When I can't find a way to pay my bills, and when man tries to find, but can't scratch my ills.

I can always look to you, my savior, and my friend.

You are the one who will walk with me until the end.

I love you, God.

I can't get enough, so fill me Lord, please fill me up.

Forgive me for putting limits on your love, boxing your blessings and sabotaging my salvation due to misplaced trust.

Forgive me.

Marcia Riggs Hawkins

Deceit

Well, here we are. The happy time when Satan comes creeping at the door.

He just loves to fish, so let's see what his bait is 'gonna be today.

Hmmm, maybe a nice argument about money, or some good lure of deception? How about a dose of mistrust, or even I hint of infidelity?

Whatever it is, he knows just what to use and how much of it to use.

Let's see if he wants a little. Maybe deception will do.

But, if he wants an all-nighter then he might just mix all of the ingredients together and make one big mess!

Satan is a great cook, and he likes all his fires hot, so he will keep all his isles on for those incidental dishes that might come his way.

He always has a special pot for those!

Don't worry because if you just have a little bit he has plenty to add to compliment any dish!

All he needs to see is a need for his fine culinary arts.

Yep, Satan is a great cook.

Be careful, so you don't end up as one of his tasty meals!

Deep Pain

Yesterday the pain cut deep in my heart.

The silly lies, transparent alibis of a lifestyle that had only been fictional to me. What was spoken in the dark became my light because that was the life I was living.

Transformations from man to beast, dancing with the demonic spirits.

Back to reality made me wonder, who, what, and where is my God?
But today the beast is a man, and the man is far from demonic.

The dance is with the Holy Spirit, you see the man switched partners from haunted to holy, from demonic to demonstrating God's love, from wanting another hit to taking a hit for the team, God's All-stars.

Tomorrow is the promise of things to come like waking up instead of creeping in, of planning our day instead of avoiding conversation, of reaping the promises instead of reaping what we sowed yesterday, today, and tomorrow.

Marcia Riggs Hawkins

The Definition of Me

To define me would be to know me. Now, I know that sounds like something you've heard before, but let me explain myself in a mysterious metaphor.
God gave me breath, the one that created my life, and in a continuous rhythm, it keeps motion like waves in the ocean. Like the beat in a song, my life has just rolled on, and from one segment to the next, as I take my next breath.
He has orchestrated, dictated, and motivated my very soul from an egg to a being from a baby to a child, a girl to a woman. I've become, and each new season in my life has brought chapters, some that my girlish mind could not capture, and others, that woman dare not speak of.
He created me in His image, and He is beautiful, so the beauty he adorns on me has been fashioned by his hand, my soul, His spirit, my God. Since He made me, only He knows me. The definition of me is him, so to know me, you must know Him, my Father, Creator of all, only with his help can I stand tall and be the woman He created me to be.
That is the definition of me.

Marcia Riggs Hawkins

Thirst Quenched: Woman at the Well

Don't Judge Me

You see my smile, my teeth, oh, so bright.

The reverse frown that you might call a smile.

The face, created just for your pleasure-- to look at, that is.

My hair, showing its versatility in style-- straight, curled, naturally worn.

My eyes are hazel, brown, and grey, depending on the season-- my season.

My body is, well, curvy and grown up in all the right places.

This seems to be pretty good— *work it gurl*.

What you don't see is that the smile covers the sadness.

The brightness of my teeth deflect away from the sparkle that my eyes have lost.

My hair is the one thing that is changeable without being changed.

My eyes have seen sadness and pain so hazel is really hazed, grey is gloom and brown is darkness.

Marcia Riggs Hawkins

My body is a result of determination gone awry, and of diets that didn't do all the work.

Before you judge me based on what you see, look past and see…

What might really be?

Erase

It's like me on paper in your life.

I'm the center of your dreams, and the apple of your eye, but oops, you made a mistake, or so you think.

You're just 'gonna erase, and keep rubbing until all evidence of me is gone.

Go back and give it a do over. Cover it with whiteout, so there's no resemblance of what was once there.

But the impression on the paper says something else.

The indention in my heart, and the hole that's left, the eraser didn't touch.

Try as you might, but my heart says, it's still there.

How do you erase the memories from my mind?

The pictures that are locked in my brain?

The days like the best date ever?
Erase means to take away, but how do you do erase the memories?

Marcia Riggs Hawkins

False Hope

How could I think even for one second that those days were gone?

Wedded bliss is how I would describe the weeks of heaven when the demon was gone.

I saw in you a man that I remembered.

A man I loved and trusted with almost my life, but the demon wouldn't hear of it, not for another minute.

Too much happiness, too much "God time."

No, I mean, "HELL NAW," he says.

I'm just 'gonna give her enough-- just enough to let her know what he could be, and what I'm 'gonna make out of him. His will, mind, being, is what he wants to direct. Like a puppet, he does all the rest.

With his actions and reactions he will govern others.

Killing two, three, or even more souls with one stone is how he likes to play. Yet I thought, just for a second, that the demon was gone.

He just stepped to the side to take a rest before he would carry on.

Feel Me

Feelin' like I can't swallow this lump in my throat.

There's pain in my flesh and a hole in my heart.

My head is full of thoughts, regrets, second chances, do overs…

They all just sit in my throat.

Maybe if I could swallow some of these then my pain wouldn't be so great.

I could move forward, bury myself in some new project…

Let the part of my mind that claims dementia have those memories.

Anything just to forget what I should've done, could've said, or not, when my mouth was so anxious to be right.

This feelin' has me not feelin' like my sexy spot that needs that touch, or those lips that pressed hard against mine.

No, I'm feelin' like a heart that's trying to pump with no blood.

Lungs that are trying to breath with no air.

Marcia Riggs Hawkins

A woman who has no feelin' but pain.
I'm feelin' like I want my man.

Please, God, let him feel me.

Thirst Quenched: Woman at the Well

The Frailty of Broken Limbs

I stepped out on a limb, full of anticipation and hope.

I had been on a long road...a bark in my life that had left me bruised;

Every time I tried to reach for something, anything to hold on to, it broke.

But not without leaving me with more scars for my heart to bear.

I was carrying too much weight, so much pain that wouldn't dissipate.

From all that I could see, it looked like a limb.

It was a limb that was just waiting for me.
I looked up to see this outstretched tree. It looked so long, and sturdy.

It was capable enough for my feet to trust, so I stepped out!

I stepped out in faith, and I stepped out in love, trust and hope.

Marcia Riggs Hawkins

I stepped out believing that this limb could balance them all and it tried to hold me all the same, but when I stepped, I carried baggage from the bark.

Baggage that felt like bricks, but the limb seemed capable of holding it.

But when I got close enough to see, I noticed the limb had wear and tear, and this would later haunt me. The distance had deceived me.

This limb, the one that invited me had baggage of its own.

How could it carry mine when it had not let go of its own? That's when I realized that I had to jump!

This promising limb was just an oversized twig, so I Jumped into the arms of Jesus!

He had carried a cross, so heavy, so unbearable, and so painfully just for me!

I didn't have to hide my baggage because he told me to come to him...just as I was!

I could give it to him because he is capable, willing and able.

Thirst Quenched: Woman at the Well

Now, I don't step out on limbs.

I step out on faith in my Savior, knowing that he is a burden bearer.

He won't break.

He is able.

God,

In our bodies resides your creation, something so wonderfully made.

From the formation of our feet to the crown of our head.

You are perfect, and you created us for perfect praise to You.

Praise, honor, and glory are due to the one who created you.

Loving Him so simply is easy to do.

Can you honor Him in all that you do?

He knows the answer, and provides the way, Jesus Christ, our Savior, from yesterday to today, and forevermore.

Going Back to Bring One Forward

To save someone I have to go back, and remembering is almost like doing it over. Going back to the past that I run from every day; revisiting visions as if it were yesterday that my strength and courage were threatened by the evil they call abuse. In order to help, I must again hurt in memories that I choose to forget.

Sista, I got to pull you thru even if it kills me. My spirit is diminished with each name, slur, slap, and yet, I went back because abnormal became my normal. Friends and close acquaintances were no longer near because he pulled me from anything that resembled who I was and who I am, so now, my dear friend, I am here to pull you back to where you once belonged.

I'm saving you by telling about me because I was you, set free only by a merciful God. See, he died for me, so I didn't have to be in that. He already did the dying, so don't let that kill you. He's got enough mercy to go around, so claim yours!

Marcia Riggs Hawkins

Thirst Quenched: Woman at the Well

Happily Ever Dreams

Happily, ever after, what does it really mean?

Sounds like something in a fairy tale, or just a dream.

I used to wish, I held out hope that one day my prince would come.

In a crowd he'd see me with his X-ray vision he'd find me.

The sunset would be ours to just ride away in. Maybe there'd be a white covered wagon, or a decorated horse. Maybe a Honda, but I'd have my choice!

He'd tell me all about myself, and how long he'd searched to find a maiden as fair as me, and then with a dashing look and a soft caress, he'd kiss me, and that would seal our fate.

Whatever life we had before we met would fade into the darkness as we took the next step. Our hearts would be one, and no longer could we be without the love we'd found, so dashing toward the rainbow we would go.

All the well-wishers in the background, and as they got smaller, our future got bigger and bigger.

Marcia Riggs Hawkins

It's my fairy tale, but when I open my eyes the colors are gone and all that remains are the words of this poem only to remind me that fairy tales are gone, and happily ever afters are only in a song.

Thirst Quenched: Woman at the Well

Harvest

Reaping the harvest that God promised me; take back what the devil stole from me.

But, God? He didn't steal it. I gave it to him.

Through my back sliding, gray self, living on the fence, not being able to be identified as a Christian by my actions, but only through my loud proclamations for all who would listen.

But God, you're still waiting on me.

I'm tired of burning the candle, smoking the pipe, sleeping in the wrong bed, playing church one day a week, and giving my true spirit to the enemy.

I'm tired God. I'm tired of saying next time I will do better.

Next time is like Russian roulette, but as long as I have breathe, I'll say it.

I'll say it until you take my breath away, and then what? I'm doomed with the God I served.

I didn't mean for it to go this far.

God, you know me!

I worked in the church.

I brought people to serve.

Marcia Riggs Hawkins

I paid my tithes, sometimes...

But, then you say, get away from me!

I never knew you!

You served the God of darkness in the light I provided for your salvation!
Stay in His harvest. It's plentiful. The devil can't steal what you don't have.

He Stepped Out of My Mind

He stepped out of my mind and came to be.

How could someone so seemingly perfect love me?

Everything I had imagined in another time when life was dark, and full of strife.

I wrote about him in my other life.

My imagination described his physique, his stride, and his daunting pride.

Even the way he would ride, Sally, ride!
Here he is like he just popped out if my mind, and yes, he's mine!

With his gentle soul and calming spirit, he's telling me, "We're 'gonna be just fine."

Somehow I believe him. My soul says it's ok.

He looks at me and says, "It's all good."

I believe that like I believe in Him.

It's not because his lips spoke it, but because my spirit received it.

I've seen lips move. You know, lip service.

They move like an animated dummy, and like a dummy, there's no spirit, no truth. Yet, I allowed myself to be deceived by something that had no heart.

When this breath of fresh air, this tall glass of water, this balm in Gilead came into my life, I said to myself, this can't be right.

I mean, he's everything I dreamed of, and I'm not asleep. He's telling me he's mine to keep.

I'm a keeper?

For every inch of his thickness, I say thank you, God!

For a smile that lights my heart, I say, my soul is happy.

For every time his arms lock me next to his chest, and I breathe in his air, I can hear Toni Braxton say, "breathe again."

For every look of love I see on his face, I say, for the first time ever, this man, God's man, my man.

Thirst Quenched: Woman at the Well

He's Waiting

He's waiting somewhere on this earth.

Deep in her thoughts there is a man who is waiting on her.
He's strong, secure, and polished in his ways.

He's waiting on her so she will never have to go astray.

Waiting for the woman he knows she can be.

Waiting for God to fulfill their destiny.
He's waiting on a woman who puts God first.

The woman that God has matured in life, refusing to fall for the okie doke.

She has taken her battle scars and turned them into beauty marks.

A woman that holds her head high, and never looks down, or back to the experiences that shaped her, but looks to the one that delivered her.

He's waiting patiently because his years have taught him that virtue.

Like a diamond goes through the fire, so shall she to become a precious woman of faith.

Marcia Riggs Hawkins

On his Eve, Adam waits.

On his Michelle, Barack waits because what God has put together, no man can put asunder.

He waits, waiting, and they will know when it's right.

Their union will be so natural without even one fight.

They've already prayed and asked God to lead and when they meet there will be nothing to impede.

She is like a cutting board, marked, and dented with scratch marks in the grain. Stained with the residue of life, and so much pain.

Like the cutting board with all the wear, she still has purpose.

To exist, live, and love again.
He's waiting, the man of God.

How I Feel

How can I say what I feel without my words turning into the very weapon formed against me? How can I be understood when I don't understand how words can be spoken for the moment, but not for the future.

Does enjoying the ride mean that after the milk is extracted from the tits of the cow and they hang, lifeless with nothing left to give, that she goes out to a pasture where the requirement is being used up?

Out to the pasture she goes, never to be of any use.
How do I really feel?

CONFUSED.

Your words are not aligning with my heart.

However, I do have a heart and it was big enough to love you.

Marcia Riggs Hawkins

It's also big enough to forgive you, and myself.

All the while knowing that what God has for me will be for me.

Hurt, Pain, Loneliness, Despair

Hurt, pain, loneliness, and despair were not made for me.

My smile was not made to be a frown.

My compassion should not be met with neglect.

My heart was not intended to be bitter.
Love is supposed to lift me.

Being in love is not supposed to burden me.

I'm supposed to view my home as a haven, a place away from the world.

The world is not supposed to come in, take a seat at my table and demand my services.

The world is not supposed to rob me of the peace God intended in my home, my space, and my heart.
No, that's not for me.

If I can't see God's presence in it, then it's not for me.

If it cannot bring out my best, then it's not for me.

If God can't be glorified in it, then it's not for me.

Marcia Riggs Hawkins

If it can't treasure and keep me the way God intended, then it's not for me.

Love lifted me, when nothing else could help.

Nothing else is for me.

I Am the Prize

I am the prize! Not because of my big luscious thighs, or these pretty brown eyes. Or my Dorothy Dandridge hips, that make you 'wanna get a grip!

Not even my natural hair that you swear it's a weave….no, baby! It's all grown in from the root, and that you can believe!

See, all this was put together, very carefully by a craftsman that only made one of me. My DNA is unique; one of a kind. So when you get me, you get the prize. His label, etched on my heart, and because he made me, we will never part. So watch how you handle his merchcandis3e, because when it's gone, the only thing you can say, is what you should've done!

Watch, guard, and handle with care, your prize.

Thirst Quenched: Woman at the Well

I Smile

I smile when I imagine your face.

I have a playback in my mind.

I go back to buttermilk pies, and the end of a lunch, abruptly interrupted.

I think about the many times your name danced in my head.

I wondered why.

Seeing you by chance, in a hallway nearby, I smile.

How was I to know my fate and my future would be intertwined in yours?

Your life, your love, and your smile.
A man so confident, everything I could want and more than I need.

Who looks at me and I blush like a girl.

Who, with the thought of his touch, my body anticipates love for the first time. Attentive to my needs, and wants, has taken my heart, and carefully placed it in a glass case, so no one can break it ever again.

Mother, they really do exist.

Knights on white horses, fairy tale dreams, and happily ever after, or maybe it's the grace of God. A God who knows, and knows.

My creator, who made me, and made my smile. He knew better than me.

He knew what being in love with you could be.
I smile because God wants me to delight in Him.

I smile because he's given me the desire of my heart.

He's allowed me to give my heart to you, so I smile.

Thirst Quenched: Woman at the Well

Lord I'm Calling on You...

These trials I just can't seem to get through.

Please help me. Show me how to ease the pain from what this life is dishing me, I've yet to gain. The storms I face seem to know me well.

When they call my name I have to yell, "Lord, Why?"

They seem to be just for me.

It's my personal storm calling on me.

When it seems like my soul has found peace, and the waves of tribulation are no more, here comes remnants of the storm before.

It never really leaves, it just hides from my fears, and when I'm feeling stronger, it lets me know, it's still here.
Tell me Lord, how to ease the pain from these personal storms that keep calling my name.

I know you can move mountains, and I heard you even calmed the sea.

Please, Lord, speak to my storm; do it for me. I'll stand on Your word. It's the only foundation I shall hold. I'm clinging to your promises just like the stories told.

Marcia Riggs Hawkins

I know my God can take away the pain from these personal storms that call my name.

Thirst Quenched: Woman at the Well

My Other Sista

You look at us with envy, your hearts full of deceit-- like you wish you could be.
Dare not say it aloud, but in front of the crowd you sneer, hiss and hate, wishing our beauty would dissipate.

You try to emulate the size of our lips, the thickness of our hips and the rhythm of our dance.

It's what our bodies were made for because our rhythm is from the motherland from which we were snatched!

Yet, in this day you still carry the torch of hate, passed down from your grandmother's grandmother from the sting of the whip to the open flesh in my back.

You tried to break us, but we didn't stumble. Now you take our mothers sons, our sister's brothers, my monkey's uncle and present yourself as the lighter version of a sista, but the soul, the essence, the very core of you will never possess.

Marcia Riggs Hawkins

It's not to be manipulated, or duplicated.

We will not capitulate who we are.
Our strength lies in our God, and as long as He is we are

STRONG, AND BEAUTIFUL

My Thickness

My thickness I embraced as an inheritance of my race as a treasured gift from those before, now known as the love handles that you adore

They are handles to carry the weight from predecessors to ancestors-my weight.

For the lost daughters, the weight for those who carried me, and the ones who didn't, and as I carry, I embrace the weight that now defines from my curvaceous hips to the stride that was made from my pride of being a woman, and woman enough!

I embrace the tests and trials that through it all, I learned to trust in Jesus.

I embrace the scars from the battles that I didn't choose to fight, but victory was mine!

I embrace the loves that I lost, and the ones that should've gotten lost because all that I've been through molded the woman that I embrace. Yeah, she's thick with hips as you please, legs that can wrap all around, and lips to call your name.

There's RHYTHM to match all of these. It makes up the experience, and as I look at it all, I embrace me.

Marcia Riggs Hawkins

Our Story

When I first saw him I didn't know what to think.

Who is this man? I wondered aloud.

He played those keys with such a beautiful stride, but how was I to know that he was dying on the inside?

I watched his gift go up and down those keys

The lord spoke to me and said, "In him I am pleased,

You will be united with him in holy matrimony."

I thought to myself, he doesn't even fit my bill,

Then God said to me, "it's not about you

It's all about my will."

We dated, and married in front of a Christmas tree.

On Christmas eve-- life seemed so perfect, for him and me.

Then life came knocking on our door...

First a knock, and then a swift kick,

I hit the floor!

"Gotta get low," my mind said. I didn't want anyone to see what these life changes were doing to me.

Not the Mary Jane, but the crack cocaine sought to destroy. What we had could not compete with that little peace pipe that he made love to every night.

What would my friends say? Would they understand?

How could being in love feel like sinking sand?

Sinking in deep water, but I can't swim.

No one really knew the pain that I was in.

Thirst Quenched: Woman at the Well

The waters were rising, and I couldn't see my feet, but only this thing they call defeat.

There might be a shore, but I couldn't see anymore.

All this mayhem kept pulling me deeper and deeper for so much more.

I told God, "I can't see my feet and with all this water, I can't be complete."

My faith was lost, drowning in my tears and fears.

What was 'gonna become of my life in just a few years?

God took me away from what was left of those ruins.

Not because I asked, but so he could do his task.

Frankly, I didn't care…Just work in my life.

Don't leave me here with all this misery and strife.

It seemed that the pipe had won, so I threw in the towel, but the separation was working on his life and mine.

It brought us back from the destruction we knew.

The test turned into a testimony of trials and victories.

I still see deep water and it sometimes makes me fear, but I know that my God is always near.

I can see my feet, when he calls me to the deep.

But, even if I can't, I know my savior can.

The next time I love, it must be unconditionally,

Christ does it for me.

Thirst Quenched: Woman at the Well

Queen

If I insist on the meal, and refuse your crumbs…

If I stand for right, and don't succumb.

If I demand your respect, and settle for nothing less…
Does that make me less of a prospect?

If my beauty fades with the passing years, and age comes to me with the evolution of time…

Does that make me less of a queen in your mind?
I am a queen with several definitions abounding in me.

My beauty, posture, and yes, the God that lives in me.

Crumbs I do not have to accept because my Father's table has plenty and room for all.

In standing with him, I stand for right, and He is the one who will always fight.

Grace I wear, and I am wearing well.

Man cannot condemn me to heaven or hell.
I am a queen in all that you see.

I am a queen.

Thirst Quenched: Woman at the Well

Reclaiming Myself

As I consider this, the rejecting flow makes me ponder and ask, why do I have to sell myself to someone that shouldn't even have to ask?

I give myself as you give to me, but then as you get your fill, you want no more of me.

See, it's all routine. It's nothing new, so I take it back. I take it all from you.

Until you understand that every moment between my love is a treasure, and not some old routine that you forgot to measure.

Every time the sea parts is another miracle from God because it was He that brought you to me, and He that consented your soul to mine.

Don't take anything for granted.

There may never be another time, so when I say, come and dine then you should step right in.

The water's always fine.

Thank You

Father,
As you've brought me to, so you've brought me through.

I can literally look back and see your hand all over my situations, my heartaches, disappointments, hurts and pain because all those things didn't kill me nor take my spirit.

Maybe some things had to happen to empty more of myself and replace it with more of You.

I thank you, God, for being merciful.

I thank you for saving me when I didn't realize how close danger was.

I thank you for the many times death looked past me.

You are a God that can fulfill seemingly impossible dreams and who can restore life to dead circumstances.

You are a God that can bring life to dead marriages, and allow love happiness after so much pain.

I thank you God, for fulfilling Your will instead of my own.

Marcia Riggs Hawkins

I thank you for the restoration you've placed in my life in Your time.

In spite of calamity you still have a plan for me, and it's working for my good

Thirst Quenched: Woman at the Well

Unconditional

I wish I had a sweetheart, someone to whom I'm true.

I wish that I had love, and that that love was you.

A man that could see, past my perfected perfectionism.

A man that could love me anyway.

A man that was my best friend.

Someone who could see past the glam, makeup and clothes.

Someone who could just see a woman, from my crown down to my toes.

Someone who could understand me, like I seek to understand others.

Someone who would pour into me as I pour into others.

He would love God more than he loved me, and I would see that he is taking me to a place worth going, a place…in Him.

He would love my body as an intricate piece of art, sculptured by our God.

I am in my Father's design to fulfill my man's desires.

He would also cherish every inch of my skin,

And every hair that lays and curls.
The love that he would have for me would blow his mind, and I'd blow his mind, that is…

How could love like this be so spiritually sexual?
Can love like this ever be?

Will it ever come to me?

Thirst Quenched: Woman at the Well

Under Construction

How many times have you driven past, or walked by a construction site?

Then looked at your own life and said,

This is my plight?

Our own situation can look like a mess.

We're living in a mess, or we are the mess,

But, God wants our best?

The physical eye sometimes cannot see what God is fashioning us to be.

His spiritual eye sees past our pain,

And loves us thru all the fallen debris and rain.

But like that construction site, there is purpose in our pain.

Those slabs of concrete become a foundation on which we stand,

And his word is true. It's not like sinking sand.

Putty and plaster become walls.

Marcia Riggs Hawkins

The panes of glass become the window to our future.

Don't despair, but lift your head high.

God is working in your life. Keep your eyes on him, and watch him work.

He will come into the construction site of your life.

He will take what he can use, and discard the rest.

It's all in the test.

Being under construction is not a bad thing when He is the developer...

The Almighty King!

Thirst Quenched: Woman at the Well

Untimely Cravings of Course

All it took was one phone call, and there you went.

There were promises made, and promises bent.

A half-eaten sandwich, lights on, doors unlocked for the world to invade; sin had already called, and took you away.
As I looked around and observed the remnants of intentional acts, I have to wonder, how to take my life back. It does not belong to you, or the pipe you adore. It does not belong for your feet to wipe as the mat at the back door.

Nor is its purpose for you to do as you please, or to sit and wait as you come back as the beast.
My life, loves, and things dear to me are not meant for your destruction, but meant for my reproduction.

From your mess, God produces miracles.

From your abuse comes Gods amazing, unfailing love for me.

From your slurs come God's wonderful promises.

From your actions come God's blessings for me.

I claim my life from you because it's not yours to claim.

Marcia Riggs Hawkins

Your blood was not shed, and there are no stripes on your back, just the monkey they call crack.

I surrender all to Jesus, including you, and you, and that.

I do all of this as I take my life back.

Thirst Quenched: Woman at the Well

When You Look at me, What Do You Really See?

(Tamir Rice)

I'm only 12 years old, out of my abode, and playing on the street while I'm dreaming of my thanksgiving treats.

It feels like my only crime was being black as the bullet hit my chest, busting out of my back.

I'm thinking, damn, I'm only 12, what did I do? Now, my life is over, and it's all because of you. When you looked at me, what did you see?

That big dude, Mike Brown, who was just shot in the streets? What did he do? That caused the trigger to pull, and caused his body to lie in his own pool, for hours and hours, helpless in his own blood.

Did you see him as a kid, or just as a thug? When you looked at Eric garner, what did you really see? A man taking care of his family, but yet, he can't breathe? The marks were against him as soon as he left his mother's womb, but it could not prepare him for his doom. He's in the ground, covered with dirt, and no one can even imagine his family's hurt.

Marcia Riggs Hawkins

When you looked at me, did you see your rage?
Did you see my many ancestors who have been trapped in your cage?

I was only 12, man, why couldn't you see? I was just a boy, and I wanted to be.

I just wanted to be, but look at me.

Thirst Quenched: Woman at the Well

Where am I?

I feel like I ain't even here especially when you're near.

The end is crystal clear. Your eyes show nuthin' there, and we both engage in blank stares because the writing's on the wall; it's really there.

Where did we go wrong, or did we ever go right? Right to the truth that time wouldn't hide. Now all I have left is my pride.

Everything was lost in the fire of desire: Candyland dreams and happily ever after. Now all I have left cannot be taken away because it's locked deep inside my heart, and no made up dream can tear us apart. He's my rock like none other.

He knew this day would come, and I'd have to look and see, and take inventory of what had become of the fantasy I thought I had. Oh, yeah, my bad.

Nothing can fill my savior's shoes, and a million of them cannot equal one of him. I can feel that familiar pain and I thought I'd never see it again. It's really hard to take it all in. But then I exhale that sigh of relief, knowing that I can lay these and other burdens at my Savior's feet.

His yoke is easy and his burden is light, so as I end this piece, I know I'm 'gonna be alright.

White Horses and Fairy Tales

White horses belong in fairy tales.

The men that rode them are locked in a time that is far away.

Only in dreams does it dare to come close.

White horses and white lies are almost the same.

They can carry you far, and if you're not careful, they'll throw you off track.

We believe until it's wrong, hope until it's lost, and dream until the sun comes,

And sheds the light on what we refuse to believe, or see.

White horses and the men who ride them are only in our dreams.

Fairy tales ain't what they used to be.

Marcia Riggs Hawkins

Thirst Quenched: Woman at the Well

Winning

I am the prize! Not because of my big luscious thighs, or these pretty brown eyes, or my Dorothy Dandridge hips that make you wanna take a grip!

Not even my natural hair that they swear is a weave. No, baby, it's all natural, home grown, and that you can believe!

See, all this was put together very carefully by a craftsman that only made one of me. My DNA is unique, it's one of a kind, and when you get me, you get the prize. His label is etched on my heart, and because he made me, we will never part, so watch how you handle is property.

Marcia Riggs Hawkins

Woman at the Well

She was a woman of many years, and many tears had fallen on her face. Tired, from the decisions in her life; tired, from shame and regret; broken, from the issues of her past.

They all led her here to this well at the noon hour that was the hottest time of the day.

Surely no one would be here, at this time…or so she thought.

There would be no one to ridicule or stare;

No man to whisper and no woman to sneer.

No one to wonder about who, or what she is.

That sounds like some of us. Makeup can hide the scars, but it can't erase the pain in your heart.

We learn to be functional in dysfunctional relationships. And by default, we learn how to manage a mess.

She doesn't come to the well empty-handed, she just comes, empty.

Her arms are loaded with pots she will fill from a well that is as deep as the anguish and pain she feels.

As she approaches, she sees a man. He looks at her, but not like the others do. He looks at her as if he can see her soul. He offers her living water….not water that she would have to reach down and get, but look up and receive!

She wondered; why is he offering me anything? Doesn't he know who or what I am? He begin to tell her about the 5 husbands she had, as well as the man that lay in her bed at the present, and yet Jesus!!

He knew about the men she had married for the moment. Jesus knew that when they met, she would become transformed…

Romans 12:2 – "do not conform to the pattern of this world, but be transformed by the renewing of your mind."

She came empty, and left full.

And so now, her past, her mistakes are all forgiven. For so long she complained about men using her, and now, all she wanted was to be used by this man, Jesus.

Thirst Quenched: Woman at the Well

He will meet us at the well of our lives. He will meet us in our pain and hurt, anguish and despair, and is ready to transform us.

Take a drink of his living water.

The Woman You Trained

This is the woman you trained me to be; full of doubt, pain and misery. You like me there, so you can manipulate, capitulate but you will never equate to what true love is.

See, God has decided to take your weapon of mass destruction, your tongue, and render it powerless. The same weapon that originated from your throat, and connects to the palate, travels in that empty space, and mixed with your spit, came hurling at me like bricks, leaving wounds with no marks...only shattered pieces of my heart.

And just like a trained soldier always on alert, my emotions have to shield this hurt. And at your command, be your baby tonight, or suffer your mouth, with no end in sight.

Yeah, that was the woman you wanted me to be, but God is not having it, as you can see. I've been recreated, again, by the one that calms my seas. He just speaks the word, and all is well. And even while was in this hell, he was with me.

I thank him for grace every chance I get...His words to me are I can, I am, and he will...positive affirmations that only he can fulfill. He is my

Marcia Riggs Hawkins

father and I am his child. I am no longer the object of one that chooses to defile.

I am because he is; not because of you. So chew on that, you silly fool.

WORDS

Words, strong and true, yet they have varying effects for different people. From some who don't mean a damn thing to me, they are simply letters formed without meaning, but just an utterance of sound, but from those that are allowed to be close to my heart, they can sting, cause an upset stomach or even literally cause my heart to ache.

Words are really like milk in the mud. Once they've left your mouth they can never be retracted, so the pain, the sting that they can cause can soon become a scar; evidence of what was said and how it felt.

Words...they say the tongue is the sharpest weapon. The tongue carries the words that cut like a knife.

What is the balm, the ointment, the salve that will heal a wound so deep?

What can heal a scar that only God can see? The blood of Jesus is the salve, or the ointment. His balm can heal the words that were meant to kill your spirit, your soul, your character and even your life.

So, sisters, watch the words you speak to each other and to yourselves. God speaks promise in his word every day. His promises can be taken to the bank of enrichment. We can take his words and his promises and transform our lives to be everything that he has already seen in us.

When you listen to words, make sure they are words that transform you in to a better you.

Thirst Quenched: Woman at the Well

Your Will/My Purpose

God help me to understand the purpose you've placed on my life.

I know that in accepting your will, I give up my own.

Sometimes I will feel like a stranger even in my own home.

Purpose my life, so that it pleases you.

Take away the things that you'd have me not to do.

Rearrange those in my life so that Your will is done.

Let me not lose one Godly soul; no, not one.

My soul wants to please you, and my heart feels the same.

My flesh gets weak, but I have no one to blame.

I keep striving and wanting to be the person, the woman, you've created me to be.

No one before you, never will I place, I need you now, please show me your grace.

Amen

Marcia Riggs Hawkins

www.ingramcontent.com/pod-product-compliance
Lightning Source LLC
Chambersburg PA
CBHW071146090426
42736CB00012B/2249